P9-BZB-894

~ ~ 2005

JAN 2 6 2005

OCT 1 9 2005
MAY 2 9 2007

SEEDS and SEEDLINGS

TEXT BY ELAINE PASCOE

PHOTOGRAPHS BY DWIGHT KUHN

BLACKBIRCH PRESS, INC.

WOODBRIDGE, CONNECTICUT

Published by Blackbirch Press, Inc.
260 Amity Road
Woodbridge, CT 06525

Printed in the United States

10 9 8 7 6 5 4 3

front cover: mixed seeds
back cover: (left to right) bean seeds, radish seed germinating, bean seed sprouting, bean seedling

Library of Congress Cataloging-in-Publication Data
Pascoe, Elaine.
Seeds and seedlings / by Elaine Pascoe. — 1st ed.
     p.   cm. — (Nature close up)
   Includes bibliographical references (p. 47) and index.
   Summary: Describes how seeds are formed, how they grow, what they look like, how they reproduce, and how they make food and provides instruction for related hands-on science projects.
   ISBN 1-56711-178-5 (alk. paper)
   1. Seeds—Juvenile literature. 2. Seeds—Experiments—Juvenile literature. 3. Seedlings—Experiments—Juvenile literature. [1. Seeds. 2. Seeds—Experiments. 3. Experiments.] I. Title. II. Series.
QK661.P27   1997   95-25178
582'.0467—dc20   CIP
                                       AC

To my sister Wanda   To S.M.S.
      –D.K.   –E.P.

Note on metric conversions: The metric conversions given in Chapters 2 and 3 of this book are not always exact equivalents of U.S. measures. Instead, they provide a workable quantity for each experiment in metric units. The abbreviations used are:
    cm   centimeter   **m**   meter

Contents

◆◆◆◆◆◆

1

From Seed to Flower

Just about anywhere you look, from fields and forests to city lots and window boxes, you can find plant seeds. Seeds are practically everywhere in nature—that is, practically everywhere that plants grow. But even though they are common, seeds are one of nature's most amazing creations.

A seed is a tiny packet that contains everything needed to make a new plant. With a little water and the right soil and growing conditions—presto! Each little golden seed inside a tomato can grow into a vine that bears dozens of new tomatoes. A huge maple tree can spring from a seed smaller than the tip of your finger. It's quite a trick!

Plants have other ways of reproducing, but seeds are the most common way. In fact, more than 230,000 different kinds of plants reproduce by making seeds. Pines and other coniferous trees carry their seeds in cones. They belong to a group of plants called gymnosperms. The seeds of other plants, called angiosperms, are contained in fruits. An acorn, an apple, an ear of corn, and the seed pod of a marigold are different kinds of fruits, even though you might not think of all of them as such. And they are all borne by flowering plants—even the acorn. It began as a tiny flower on an oak tree.

Seeds vary almost as much as plants do. They come in all shapes—round and fat, long and thin, smooth or ridged—and all sizes. The size of a seed often has no relation at all to the size of the plant that grows from it. Bean seeds, pumpkin seeds, and watermelon seeds are large, but they produce low-growing vines. Towering pines and firs grow from very tiny seeds.

5

Biggest and Smallest

The biggest seeds are coconuts—the seeds of coconut palms. Certain kinds can weigh more than 20 pounds (about 9 kg). Some of the smallest seeds are produced by poppy and tobacco plants. These seeds are as small as grains of sand—you could carry thousands in your hand, and it would take millions to equal the weight of a coconut.

The pistil and stamens are visible in this lily.

How Seeds Form

Seeds begin with flowers. In the heart of a flower, surrounded by petals, are some special structures—the plant's reproductive organs. At the center is the pistil (or sometimes several pistils). The pistil is the female part of the flower. It is made up of a long neck and a round base, called the ovary. The ovary contains tiny ovules, which will one day develop into seeds. But that will happen only if they are fertilized by pollen.

Pollen is produced by the stamens, the male part of the flower. Some plants have only male or only female flowers, but the flowers of most plants have both male and female parts. The stamens surround the pistil, forming a ring of thin stalks. The tips of the stamens are covered with pollen, and if you touch them, some of this fine powder will come off on your fingertips.

Tomato flower

Flower with developing fruit

Ovary becomes fruit

Ripe tomato

Seeds inside tomato

For seeds to form, pollen must reach an ovule. This happens when a grain of pollen lands on the tip of the pistil. The pollen may come from the same flower. This is called self-pollination. Or it may be carried—by the wind or by insects, birds, or other animals—from another flower of the same type of plant. This cross-pollination helps produce strong, healthy new plants by mixing the heredity of different parent plants. Many of the features of flowers—their beautiful petals, bright colors, sweet scents, and sugary nectar—are designed to attract insects and other visitors who may carry pollen from flower to flower.

When a grain of pollen falls on the sticky tip of the pistil, the pollen swells. Soon, it begins to grow a long tube that reaches down through the neck of the pistil to the ovary, where it joins with an ovule. The ovule is fertilized, and a seed begins to form.

As seeds develop inside, the ovary itself changes. It becomes the fruit of the plant. It may swell into a soft, fleshy fruit, such as a banana, a pear, or a tomato. It may form a hard shell or husk, like the shell of a walnut or a coconut. Or it may become a dry pod, like a bean pod.

Far left: The seed of a corn plant is an example of a monocot.
Left: A bean is an example of a dicot.

Inside a Seed

Seeds may come in many shapes and sizes, but they all have the same basic parts. Inside the outer layer, or seed coat, is a tiny embryo that will develop into a new plant. The seed also contains a supply of food that will nourish the new plant when it starts to grow.

The food supply takes up most of the seed. It's a starchy material that's stored in areas of the seed called the endosperm and the cotyledons, or seed leaves. Some plant seeds, such as corn kernels, have a single cotyledon. These plants are called monocotyledons, or monocots. The seeds of most flowering plants have two cotyledons. These plants are dicotyledons, or dicots.

If you soak a bean seed in water overnight, you'll be able to split the two cotyledons apart and look inside the seed. The embryo looks like a very tiny plant. At one end is the bud that will grow into the plant's stem and leaves. The opposite end will grow to form its roots.

How Seeds Grow

Seeds seem lifeless, but they are really just sleeping, or dormant. They wake up and start to grow, or germinate, only when conditions are right. For growth, seeds must have oxygen, moisture, and warmth. But not all seeds need the same amounts of these things. Some seeds must have a great deal of moisture; others need much less. Some will sprout when the ground has barely thawed in spring. Others won't come up until the soil is thoroughly warmed.

Seeds also need good timing to sprout. The seeds of some plants, such as the willow tree, die within a few days if they do not find the right conditions. But most seeds are dormant for several months before they sprout. Seeds that are more than a year old are less likely to germinate. Wheat seeds, however, have been known to sprout after 30 years, and in experiments some weed seeds have sprouted after 50 years!

When a seed lands in the right spot, at the right time, with the right conditions, it begins to soak up moisture from the ground. The moisture makes it swell, and it soon breaks out of its seed coat. Then the embryo begins to grow. Tiny root hairs spread out, anchoring the plant and pulling in moisture and nutrients from the soil. The embryo straightens, and a seedling pops out of the earth.

Tiny root hairs anchor a sprouting plant.

9

The food stored in the cotyledons provides all the energy that the plant needs for this first burst of growth. In some plants, such as beans, the cotyledons are carried above the ground, but in others they stay below the soil. As soon as the seedling emerges, it begins to grow its first true leaves. Once the plant leafs out, it will be able to make its own food, using the energy in sunlight.

The leaves also allow the plant to breathe. Plants take in carbon dioxide from the air and release oxygen—just the opposite of what you do when you breathe. Air enters through tiny pores called stomates on the undersides of the leaves. The stomates also release excess water vapor. But when a plant starts to dry out, the stomates close up to keep water inside.

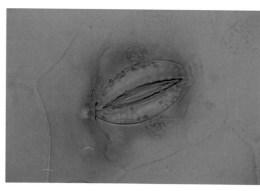

Far left: At first, food stored in the cotyledon fuels the plant. Later, sunlight enables it to make energy. *Left*: Stomates in leaves open to take in air and to release moisture.

10

Food Factories

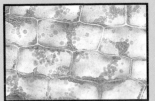

Plants make their own food out of water and air, which they take in through their roots and leaves. They do this through photosynthesis, one of the most important chemical processes on Earth. Inside the cells of plant leaves are chemicals called pigments that can absorb the energy of sunlight. Chlorophyll, which gives plants their green color, is the most important of these pigments. The small green bodies visible in the photo above are chloroplasts—the sites of photosynthesis. The plant uses solar energy captured by chlorophyll to turn water and carbon dioxide (a gas present in the air) into glucose, a sugar that nourishes the plant. Then, the plant releases the waste product of this process—oxygen, which people and other animals need to live. Except for a few types of tiny one-celled organisms, only plants make their own food. They are the first step in the food chain that keeps all living things alive.

While the stem and leaves grow up, the plant's roots continue to grow down. Depending on the type of plant, it may form a branching root system or a deep, central tap root—a thick root where food is stored. A carrot is an example of a tap root. Eventually, the plant produces flowers and seeds of its own, starting the cycle again.

Right: This pumpkin plant has a branching root system.
Far right: Carrots are tap roots.

How Seeds Travel

If a maple tree dropped all its seeds on the ground right beneath its branches, few of them would grow into new trees. It would be too shady under the parent tree, and the little maple seedlings would crowd each other out. The maple solves this problem by giving its seeds wings. Equipped with stiff flaps that catch the breeze, each pair of maple seeds rides away from the tree on the wind.

Nearly all seed-bearing plants have some method of spreading their seeds. Many, like the maple, use the wind. Dandelion and milkweed seeds have fluffy white parachutes. Very small seeds, like those of poppies and orchids, are so light that they can be carried by the breeze without any special structures. Other plants give their seeds a push. When the seed pods of violets, witch hazel, and certain other plants are ripe, they pop open, and the seeds fly out in all directions.

Inset: **Dandelions have seeds like fluffy white parachutes.**
Left: **Maple seeds have stiff flaps that catch the breeze and carry them far from the tree.**

Plants that live near water may use it to spread their seeds. These seeds often have air-filled spaces inside so that they float. Coconuts, for example, can bob along for miles in the ocean.

If you walk through a field in late summer, you'll probably help plants scatter their seeds. Burdock seeds, cockleburs, beggar-ticks, and many other seeds have spines and hooks that latch onto passing animals—and clothing—to get a free ride to a new location.

Birds and other animals help scatter seeds by eating fruits, too. Birds carry off fruits such as berries, eat the fleshy parts, and discard the hard seeds. Squirrels and chipmunks are great seed spreaders. They hide nuts and other seeds, but they don't always return to eat them. Those that are left may sprout.

Of course, a great many seeds are eaten, by birds and other animals as well as squirrels. Many more fall in places where they can't sprout because conditions aren't right. But most plants produce many, many seeds—so there are always some that grow.

New Plants Without Seeds

Some plants can reproduce without seeds. Even some plants that make flowers and seeds can reproduce without them. Here are some examples.

Top left: The strawberry is one of many plants that send out long horizontal stems called runners. New plants pop up along the runners.

Top right: Cuttings from certain plants will grow roots in water. The cutting can then be put in soil, and a new plant will grow. Peperomia, a common houseplant, is one of these.

Bottom left: A potato sprouts new shoots and roots from the "eyes" on in its surface. One potato can produce several new plants this way.

Bottom right: The kalanchoe, another common houseplant, produces tiny new plants along the edges of its leaves. When these fall off, they take root in the soil.

2

Growing Plants from Seeds

It's easy and fun to grow plants from seeds. All you need to do is make sure that the conditions are right for growth. Then the seeds take over.

You can grow seeds that you collect outdoors. But you will have the best success with seeds that are sold in packets at garden centers or through the mail. These have been chosen and handled carefully to make sure that most will sprout.

Make sure that seeds you buy have not been treated with chemicals. Some seeds, for example, are treated with fungicides to prevent the growth of mold. The fungicide forms a powdery coating on the seeds. If you are not sure if seeds have been treated, ask before you buy them.

This chapter will give you some basic guidelines for planting seeds and raising seedlings. Remember, however, that different types of plants need different conditions. Seed packets carry specific instructions for planting the seeds inside.

Some plants are very demanding—they must have just the right soils and temperatures. Others are not so picky, and these are easier to grow. Beans, radishes, gourds, pumpkins, sunflowers, marigolds, and nasturtiums are plants that you may especially enjoy growing from seeds.

What You Need:

* A sunny spot for planting
* Spade or shovel
* Rake or garden cultivator
* Seeds
* Watering can or hose with fine spray nozzle
* Compost or peat moss (optional)

Planting Seeds in the Garden

The seeds of many fast-growing plants—like those listed on page 16—can be planted right in the garden. Big, sturdy seeds, such as bean seeds, are especially easy. You can give big seeds a head start on growth by soaking them in water overnight before planting.

What to Do:

1. If you are making a new garden, dig up the soil to a depth of 8 inches (about 20 cm). Take out all the weeds and stones, and break up clumps of soil.
2. To make the garden ready for seeds, use a rake or cultivator to break up the top 2 inches (about 5 cm) of soil into fine particles. For best results, mix in some compost or peat moss, which you can buy at a garden center. Then, rake the surface smooth.
3. Plant your seeds in rows. That way, when your seeds and weeds sprout at the same time, you'll know which are which! Space the rows about a foot (about 30 cm) apart, unless your seed packet has different instructions.
4. For each row, use a stick or a hoe to make a groove, or furrow, for the seeds. As a rule, the furrow should be twice as deep as the seeds are thick. For example, nasturtium seeds are about 1/4 inch (about .5 cm) thick, so they need a furrow 1/2 inch (about 1 cm) deep. Lima bean seeds are bigger and need a furrow about 1 inch (2–3 cm) deep. Check seed packets for specific directions.

5. Put the seeds in the furrows, spacing them according to the directions on the packet. Don't sow them too thickly—they will need space when they sprout.
6. Cover the seeds with fine soil, and pat the soil down gently. If you plant several types of seeds in your garden, label each row so you'll remember what is where.
7. Water the garden with a watering can or hose with a gentle spray nozzle—you don't want to blast the seeds out of the ground with a jet of water. Keep the soil moist, but not soggy, while you are waiting for the seeds to sprout.
8. When the seedlings come up and begin to grow true leaves, thin them out. Otherwise, they won't have enough room to grow. Seed packets usually tell you how closely the plants should be spaced. As a rule, flowers such as marigolds need 8 to 10 inches (20–25 cm) between plants, but bigger plants need more space. You can cut extra seedlings off at the soil. Or you can pull them up roots and all.

Planting Seeds in Containers

Seeds can be started in containers. After the plants begin to grow, transplant—or move—them outside to the garden or to a larger container, such as a planter or a window box.

Start seeds in flower pots, coffee cans, plastic drink cups or egg cartons, margarine tubs, or drink cartons—just about any sort of container. The containers must be clean, and they must have drainage holes. If your containers don't have holes, ask an adult to help you punch some small holes in the bottom before you begin. Soak large seeds in water overnight for a quick start.

What You Need:

* Good garden soil or sterile planting mix from a garden center
* Containers (see above)
* Seeds
* Spray bottle or plant mister
* Clear plastic bag or sheet (optional)

What to Do:

1. Fill the containers with soil or planting mix to within an inch (a couple of centimeters) of the top. Planting mix is best because it is free of weed seeds and molds that could harm your seeds.
2. Put seeds on top of the soil. If your containers are large enough, put several seeds in each, spacing them about an inch (a couple of centimeters) apart.
3. Add a top layer of soil or planting mix, to a depth twice the thickness of the seeds. If you are planting more than one type of seed, label the containers to show which is where.

4. Moisten the soil with water, using a fine spray. Keep the soil moist, but not soggy. To keep it from drying out, you can put the containers under plastic until the seeds sprout.

5. Put the containers in a place where temperatures will be between 65 and 75 degrees Fahrenheit (18°–24° C). They should have light, but direct sunlight may warm the soil too much. Set them on a tray or another surface that won't be harmed by draining water.

6. When the seeds sprout, remove the plastic. Gradually move the containers into full sunshine. Keep the soil moist.

7. The seedlings can be transplanted when they have their second set of true leaves. Lift them out of the container, roots, soil, and all, with a spoon or a small trowel. Plant them at the same depth as before, and use your fingers to firm the soil around them. Water them well.

A Tipi Garden

Gardens aren't always planted in rows. Here's a garden with a surprise—a secret hideout among the vegetables. Small pumpkins (Baby Bear and Jack Be Little varieties), pole beans, and scarlet runner beans were planted in this garden. You could try other vegetable or flowering vines—gourds, moonflowers, morning glories, and sweet peas, for example.

What You Need:

* Five poles, each 7 to 8 feet (2–2.5 m) long—sticks or any sort of pole will do)
* Rope or strong twine
* String or wide-mesh garden netting (the type sold to protect plants from deer will work)
* Spade or shovel
* Rake or garden cultivator
* Watering can or hose with fine spray nozzle
* Compost or peat moss (optional)
* Seeds of climbing plants (see above)

What to Do:

1. Choose a sunny place, and prepare the ground for planting. (See "Planting Seeds in the Garden" on page 18.)
2. Lay your poles on the ground in a bunch, and tie them together at one end with the rope or twine.
3. Stand the sticks up, and spread them out to form a tipi frame. The base of the tipi should be at least 6 feet (1.8 m) across. The wider it is, the sturdier the tipi will be.

4. To give climbing plants support, tie lengths of string between the poles. Or cover the tipi with garden netting. Leave an opening for a doorway.

5. Plant your seeds around the base of the tipi. (See "Planting Seeds in the Garden.") When shoots are long enough, start them up the frame by tying them very loosely to it or looping them through the supports. The vines' own tendrils will soon take over and anchor them to the tipi.

Vines grow up to cover the tipi frame.

3

Investigating Seeds and Seedlings

What parts of seeds and young plants are most important? What do seeds need to grow? How can you help them grow better? Here are some activities and experiments that will help you find answers to these and other questions.

What Do Seeds Need for Growth?

Can seeds grow without water? Without light? How do different temperatures affect them? Decide what you think, based on what you've read about seeds. Then try these activities to find out!

What You Need:

* Two saucers
* Paper towels
* Radish seeds
* Water mister

How Does Water Affect Seed Growth?

What to Do:

1. Soak the radish seeds in water overnight.
2. Dampen several paper towels and put them in one saucer. Put dry paper towels in the other.
3. Put radish seeds in both saucers. Keep the damp saucer moist by spraying it with the water mister. Don't spray the other saucer.

Results: Note how many seeds sprout in each container.

Conclusion: Which seeds germinate best? What does that tell you about the role of water?

How Does Air Affect Seed Growth?

What You Need:
* Two small bowls
* Pea seeds
* Paper towels
* Water mister

What to Do:
1. Soak the pea seeds in water overnight.
2. Line both bowls with paper towels. Place some seeds in each bowl.
3. Fill one container with water. Air will not be able to reach these seeds. Keep the seeds in the second container moist with the water mister, but do not let water cover them—air should reach these seeds.

Results: Note which seeds grow best.

Conclusion: What do your results tell you about the role of air? Do you think air reaches seeds when they are planted in the ground?

How Does Temperature Affect Seed Growth?

What to Do:

1. Soak the bean seeds in water overnight.
2. Line both containers with moist paper towels. Put some bean seeds in each. To keep the containers from drying out, partly cover them with plastic wrap.
3. Put one container in a warm room. Place the other container in a cool place—outdoors, if the weather is cool, or in a refrigerator.
- Note: Make sure that the containers stay equally moist and receive the same amount of light. If you put one in the refrigerator, put the other in a cupboard or under a box, such as shoe box, so that it will not receive more light.

Results: Watch the containers to see which seeds grow best.

Conclusion: Which conditions do seeds prefer—warm or cool?

What You Need:
* Bean seeds
* Two containers
* Paper towels
* Plastic wrap (optional)

What You Need:

* Radish seeds
* Paper towels
* Two saucers
* Two bowls—one clear and one solid colored (opaque)
* Water mister

What to Do:

1. Soak the radish seeds in water overnight.
2. Line saucers with moist paper towels. Put some radish seeds in each.
3. Cover one saucer with the clear bowl. Cover the other saucer with the opaque bowl.
4. Put the dishes together in a warm, bright place. Mist them with water if the paper towels begin to dry out.

Results: Note which seeds sprout faster and which seedlings grow better. Do the seedlings in the two saucers look different?

Conclusion: What do your results tell you about the role of light in plant growth?

How Important Are Seed Leaves?

The embryo is the part of the seed that actually develops into a plant. How important are the seed leaves, or cotyledons, which make up most of the seed? What will happen if they are removed? Make a prediction based on what you know about seeds. Then, do either of these experiments to see if you are right.

What Happens If Seed Leaves Are Removed Before Planting?

What to Do:

1. Soak the bean seeds in water overnight. Soak more than you think you'll need, in case some are damaged when you cut them.

2. After the seeds have soaked, put one aside. Ask an adult to help you cut the others as follows:

   • Split one seed in half, using your fingernails to carefully pull apart the two cotyledons. Keep the half with the embryo and discard the other half.

   • Divide a second seed the same way, and ask a grown-up to help cut away half of the cotyledon from the embryo.

   • Split a third seed, carefully remove the embryo, and discard the rest.

What You Need:

* Lima bean or string bean seeds
* Peat moss or peat-moss planting mix
* Seed-starting containers (one large container or four small containers)
* Knife

3. Plant the whole seed and each of the parts in your containers, following the directions in Chapter 2. Cover the seed and seed parts with about an inch (2–3 cm) of peat moss or mix. Label each of them.

4. Keep the containers equally moist and place them together in a brightly lit spot. Move them into sun when sprouts appear.

Results: When sprouts begin to come up, keep a record of their growth. What differences do you see after a week? Two weeks?

Conclusion: What do your results tell you about the different parts of seeds?

What You Need:

* Three cups or other containers
* Nine bean seeds
* Peat moss or peat-moss planting mix
* Scissors

Top: Both cotyledons have been removed.
Middle: Just one cotyledon has been removed.
Bottom: None of the cotyledons have been removed.

What Happens If Seed Leaves Are Removed After Sprouting?

What to Do:

1. Plant three bean seeds in each container, following the directions in Chapter 2. Cover them with about an inch (2–3 cm) of peat moss or mix. (Don't use fertilizer or a fertilized soil.) Put the containers in a warm, bright place, and keep them equally moist.
2. When the seeds sprout, remove all but the sturdiest seedling in each container.
3. Cut both cotyledons off the seedling in one container. Cut one cotyledon off the seedling in the second container. Leave both cotyledons on the seedling in the third container.

Results: Measure the height of the three seedlings each day and record your results.
Conclusion: Which plants grew best? Can you explain why?

Do Plants Know Up from Down?

Stems grow up, and roots grow down. But what if you turn seeds upside down—will the roots grow up and the stem down? Make a prediction, and then do this.

What to Do:

1. Cut a piece of construction paper long enough to wrap around the jar and just wide enough to fit between the base and the neck of the jar.
2. Roll the construction paper loosely. Slide it into the jar, and press it out against the sides.
3. Mist the paper to dampen it thoroughly.
4. Put seeds between the jar sides and the paper, spacing them around the jar. Place some right side up, some on their sides, and some bottom up. Use a pencil, the handle of a spoon, or your fingers to push the seeds into place. Press the damp paper back against the side of the jar.
5. Put the jar in a warm, bright place. Don't let the paper dry out.
6. After the seeds sprout, watch to see which way the roots and shoots are growing. Then, turn the jar upside down and wait a few days.

Results: Which way did the roots and shoots grow at first? Did the way that the seeds were placed make a difference? What happened after the jar was turned over?

Conclusion: What do your results tell you about plant growth? Can you think of a reason why the shoots and roots grew as they did?

What You Need:

* Small container
* Garden soil or potting soil
* Bean seeds
* Shoe box
* Tape
* Cardboard
* Scissors

Can Plants Grow Around Obstacles?

In nature, seeds may land anywhere. Seedlings may not have enough space or the right conditions, but they will always try to grow. How does a plant react when something blocks its growth? This activity will help you find out.

What to Do:

1. Plant several bean seeds in a small container, following the directions in Chapter 2. Put the container in a warm, bright place, and keep the soil moist. When the beans sprout, cut off all but the sturdiest seedling.

2. Cut a large opening in one side of the shoe box. Cut a piece of cardboard wide enough to fit the depth of the box and long enough to reach about two thirds of the way across it. Tape it in place as shown in the photo to the right.

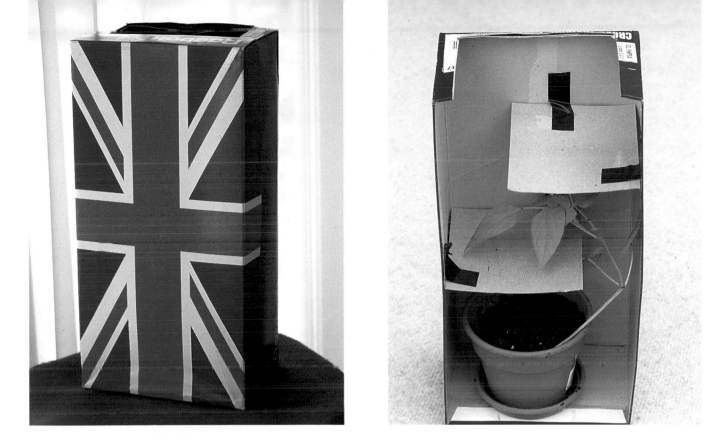

3. Put the plant in the box, under the cardboard barrier. Replace the cover, and put the box under bright light—sunlight or a plant-growing light.

4. Check the seedling daily to see how the plant is growing; keep the soil moist.

Results: What happens to the seedling as it reaches the cardboard? When the seedling clears the barrier, add a second barrier on the opposite side, farther up in the box (see photo above right). Replace the cover, and put the box back in the light. How does the new barrier affect the plant's growth?

Conclusion: Can you think of reasons why the bean plant grew as it did?

Will Fertilizer Help Seedlings Grow?

Fertilizers are added to the soil to increase the amounts of minerals and other plant nutrients. How important are those nutrients to seedlings?

What to Do:

1. Wet the sponges thoroughly, and sprinkle grass seed over them.
2. Place each sponge in a saucer, and put the saucers in a warm, bright place. Keep the sponges moist by adding water to the saucers.

3. After the seeds sprout, move the saucers into the sun. Continue to add plain water to one saucer. Keep the other saucer watered, too, but once a week add fertilizer, mixed according to the package directions.

Results: Do you see differences in the seedlings in the two saucers? Record your results over a period of time.

Conclusion: What do the results tell you about the role of plant nutrients? Would your results be different if the plants grew in soil instead of on sponges? Try it and see.

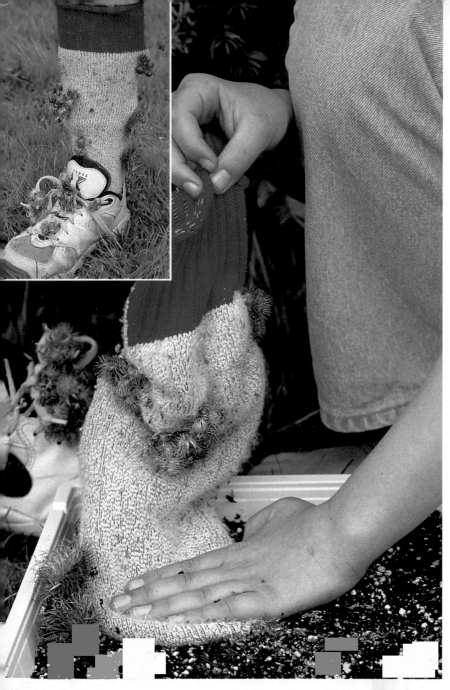

More Seed Activities

1. How many different kinds of tree seeds can you find? Take a walk through your yard or your neighborhood to see. Sort the seeds you find into categories: fruits, pods, nuts, cones, catkins, seeds with wings. Look in the kitchen for other kinds of seeds.

2. Pick up some seedy hitchhikers! Pull tall socks over your pant legs, and take a walk through a field. Then, brush the soil from your shoes and the debris on your socks onto a sheet of light paper. (Be sure to check your skin and clothing carefully for ticks or other insects that may also have hitched a ride.) Sort the seed by type. How many kinds are there?

   Plant the seeds. You can do this right away, but you may have better results if you wait a few weeks because many seeds need a period of rest, or dormancy, before sprouting. You can keep them in a cool, dry place, such as a refrigerator or a cool basement. Plant them in a flat container filled with sterile planting mix. Then, water, fertilize, and see what comes up. You can transplant the young plants into your garden when they are 2 to 4 inches (5–10 cm) tall. Can you identify the plants? How many kinds are there?

3. Did you know that plant roots are strong enough to break boulders? It's true. Look for signs of this near your home. Young plant roots grow under sidewalks or through tiny cracks in stones. As the roots grow bigger and thicker, they can break stones apart and lift the pavement up.

4. When you see their strength, it's hard to believe how delicate plant roots are. Check them out for yourself. Put some radish seeds on a moist paper towel. Cover them with another damp towel, and keep them moist with a mister. When roots have grown about half an inch (about 1 cm) long, study them with a magnifying glass. Can you see the root hairs? How do they help the plant?

5. Plants can't walk, but they can move—and you can make them do it with light.

- Grow any kind of seedling. Then, place a strong light source, such as a high intensity lamp, to one side. After a few days, check to see how the plant has responded.
- Move the lamp to other locations—directly above the seedling, to the other side, or below it, with the light shining up. How does the plant react?

6. Turn a pit into a plant. Seeds of oranges, lemons, and other citrus fruits will sprout if you soak them overnight and plant them, following the directions in Chapter 2. Planted in pots, the seedlings will grow into small trees.

Or grow an avocado tree:

- Remove an avocado seed from the fruit, and carefully peel away the papery outer covering.
- Stick several toothpicks around the middle of the seed, and set it on the rim of a glass. Add water until the bottom third of the seed is covered. Put the glass in a shaded place, away from direct light, and keep the water at that level.
- You may not see any change for several weeks, but be patient. In a while, roots will grow down into the water, and new shoots will spring up. Then, you can plant your avocado in a pot with soil and move it to a warm, sunny place.

7. Grow sprouts for salad. Use the seeds of any of these plants: alfalfa, carrots, clover, lentils, lettuce, lima beans, mung beans, oats, parsley, peas, radishes, rye, soybeans, sweet corn, or wheat. Be sure that they are not treated with chemicals.

- Put the seeds in the bottom of a glass or plastic container, and cover the top of the container with a clean piece of cheesecloth, a patch of fine nylon netting, or pantyhose. Secure the covering with a rubber band. Use separate containers for different types of seeds.
- Soak the seeds in water, and then drain the water through the netting.
- Put the container in a warm, dark place. Several times a day, add water and pour it off again. Make sure that the water drains off completely—the seeds will rot if they sit in water.
- When the seeds sprout, you can eat them in salads and stir-fried dishes. Put the container in the refrigerator to stop the sprouts' growth and keep them tasting fresh.

Results and Conclusions

Here are some possible results and conclusions for the activities on pages 24 to 37. Because so many conditions affect the way plants grow, you may not get the same results. If your outcomes differ, think about the reasons. What do you think led to your results? Repeat the activity, and see if the outcome is the same.

What Do Seeds Need for Growth?

Water, air, and warmth are all important for germination, the beginning of seed growth. (Even underground, there is enough air trapped between soil particles.) Seeds generally do not need light to germinate. But when seedlings begin to grow, they must have light so that they can begin to make their own food.

These pale sprouts were kept in the dark.

Light allowed these sprouts to turn green.

How Much of a Seed Is Needed to Make a New Plant?

The embryo needs the food stored in the rest of the seed for its first burst of growth. The more you cut away, the less well it will grow.

How Important Are Seed Leaves?

Food stored in the cotyledons, or seed leaves, provides all the energy a seedling will get until its true leaves appear. When the cotyledons are removed, the plant grows less well. If both cotyledons are removed very early, it may not survive.

Do Plants Know Up from Down?

No matter which way seeds are turned—before or after sprouting—stems grow up and roots grow down. There are two reasons. First, plants are sensitive to Earth's gravity, the pulling force that keeps your feet on the ground. The tug of gravity tells them which way their roots and shoots should go. Second, plants grow toward light. Once a shoot pops up from the soil, it reaches for the sun.

Can Plants Grow Around Obstacles?

Plants will grow toward light if there is any way to do it. They will squeeze through tiny cracks and bend in all sorts of odd shapes if they need to.

Will Fertilizer Help Seedlings Grow?

The nutrients in soil are not very important for seed germination, or even for the first burst of plant growth, because seeds carry their own food supply. As seedlings begin to grow, however, soil nutrients become very important. Gardeners add nutrients to soil with chemical fertilizers or with natural materials, such as compost and manure.

Opposite: **Plant roots always know which way is down.**

Some Words About Seeds and Seedlings

angiosperms: Plants with seeds carried in fruits.

chlorophyll: A green pigment that helps plants capture the energy in sunlight.

compost: A mixture of decaying plant matter.

coniferous: Cone bearing.

cotyledons: Seed leaves, which store food for the seed's first growth.

cross-pollination: Transfer of pollen from one plant to the ovary of another.

dicotyledons: Plants with two cotyledons.

dormant: Inactive.

embryo: The part of a seed that will form a new plant.

endosperm: The part of a seed where food is stored.

food chain: A group of living things that depend each other for food. Plants, which are eaten by animals, are at the bottom of the food chain.

germinate: Begin to grow.

gymnosperms: Plants with seeds not contained in fruits.

monocotyledons: Plants with one cotyledon.

nutrients: Materials that plants need to live and grow.

ovary: The base of the pistil, containing the ovules.

ovules: A plant's female sex cells (eggs), which develop into seeds when fertilized by pollen.

photosynthesis: The process by which plants make their own food.

pistil: The female part of a flower.

pollen: A plant's male sex cells (sperm), released as a fine powder.

self-pollination: Transfer of a plant's own pollen to its ovules.

stamens: The male parts of a flower.

stomates: Tiny pores on the undersides of leaves, through which oxygen, carbon dioxide, and water vapor pass.

Sources for Seeds

You can buy seeds at garden centers and hardware and home supply stores. Check to make sure that the seeds have not been treated with fungicides or other chemicals. You can also order untreated seeds through the mail. These companies provide catalogs:

Burpee Seeds
300 Park Avenue
Warminster, PA 18991
800-888-1447

Johnny's Selected Seeds
Foss Hill Road
Albion, ME 04910
207-437-4301

Shepherd's Garden Seeds
300 Irene Street
Torrington, CT 06790
203-482-3638

For Further Reading

Bates, Jeffrey. *Seeds to Plants: Projects with Biology.* New York: Franklin Watts, 1991.

Gibbons, Gail. *From Seed to Plant.* New York: Holiday House, 1991.

Handelsman, Judith F. *Gardens from Garbage: How to Grow Indoor Plants from Recycled Kitchen Scraps.* Brookfield, CT: Millbrook, 1993.

Kuhn, Dwight. *More Than Just a Vegetable Garden.* Englewood Cliffs, NJ: Silver Burdett, 1990.

Lerner, Carol. *Plant Families.* New York: Morrow, 1989.

Stidworthy, John. *Plants and Seeds.* New York: Franklin Watts, 1990.

Taylor, Barbara. *Growing Plants.* New York: Franklin Watts, 1991.

Index

Note: Page numbers in italics indicate pictures.